CAP
Respect
Contemporary
A Cappella Songbook

SSAA Series

A Cappella Arrangements by
Deke Sharon &
Anne Raugh

AF349103

EXCLUSIVELY DISTRIBUTED BY
HAL•LEONARD®
CORPORATION
7777 W. BLUEMOUND RD. P.O. BOX 13819 MILWAUKEE, WI 53213

TABLE OF CONTENTS

Cover photo: Jolanda Porter, Tufts *Essence*
© 2004 Mainely A Cappella

Respect

Arrangement by
Anne Raugh

Words and Music by
Otis Redding

What you need You know I got it.
I ain't gon-na do you wrong 'Cause I don't wan - na.
hoo
hoo
dm bm bah dm bm bm bah dm bm bah dm bm bm bah
All I'm ask - in' is for a lit - tle re -
hoo
hoo
dm bm bah dm bm bm bah dm bm bah dm bm bm bah
spect, when you come home. Ba - by, when you come home,
oo, just a lit - tle bit, wah oo, just a lit - tle bit, wah
dm bm bah dm bm bm bah dm bm bm bah dah dm
Re - spect.
oo, just a lit - tle bit, wah oo, just a lit - tle bit, wah
dm bm bah dm bm bm bah dm bm bm bah dah dm

15
I'm out to give you all of my mon-ey,
Ooh, your kiss-es, sweet-er than hon-ey,
oo hoo wah oo wah oo hoo wah oo wah
dm bm bah dm bm bm bah dm bm bah dm bm bm bah
But all I'm ask-in' in re-turn, hon-ey,
But guess what, so here's my mon-ey,
oo hoo wah oo wah oo hoo wah oo wah
dm bm bah dm bm bm bah dm bm bah dm bm bm bah
Is to give me my prop-er re-spect when you get
All I want you to do for me is give me some here when you get
oo hoo wah oo wah oo hoo wah oo
dm bm bah dm bm bm bah dm bm bah dm bm bm bah
21
home. Yeah, ba-by, when you get
home. Yeah, ba-by, when you get
just a, just a, just a, just a, just a, just a, just a, just a,
re, re, re, re, re, re, re, re, re-
dm bm bah dm bm bm bah dm bm bm bah dah dm

4

home.
home.

oo, just a lit - tle bit, wah oo, just a lit - tle bit, wah
spect, just a lit - tle bit, wah oo, just a lit - tle bit, wah

dm bm bah dm bm bm bah dm bm bm bah dah dm

25

R - E - S - P - E - C - T, find out what it means to me,

oo wah oo wah

oo wah oo wah

R - E - S - P - E - C - T, take care, T - C - B,

oo wah oo wah

oo wah oo wah

29 Vamp for solo
Solo ad lib.

alternate various accompaniment patterns for extended solo

sock it to me, sock it to me, sock it to me, sock it to me,

dm bm bah dm bm bm bah

sock it to me, sock it to me, sock it to me, sock it to me,
dm bm bm bah dah dm
oo, just a lit - tle bit, wah oo, just a lit - tle bit, wah
dm bm bah dm bm bm bah dm bm bm bah dah dm
ff
R - E - S - P - E - - C - - T
ff
R - E - S - P - E - - C - - T
ff
R - E - S - P - E - - C - - T

Sentimental Journey

Arrangement by
Anne Raugh

Words and Music by
Bud Green, Les Brown and Ben Homer

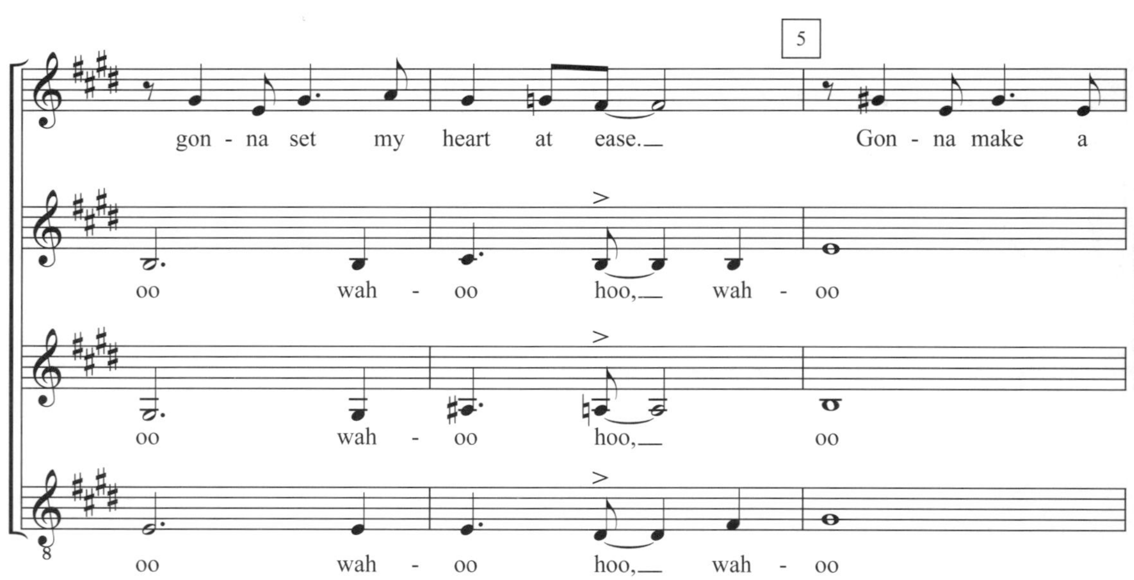

sen - ti - men - tal jour - ney to re - new old mem - o - ries.
sen - ti - men - tal, hoo old mem - o - ries.
sen - ti - men - tal, hoo old mem - o - ries.
sen - ti - men - tal, hoo old mem - o - ries. wah -

9 lightly, percussive
choo choo ch choo choo choo choo ch choo choo
mf
Got my bag, I got my res - er - va - tion,
mf
Got my bag, I got my res - er - va - tion,
mf
oo wah -

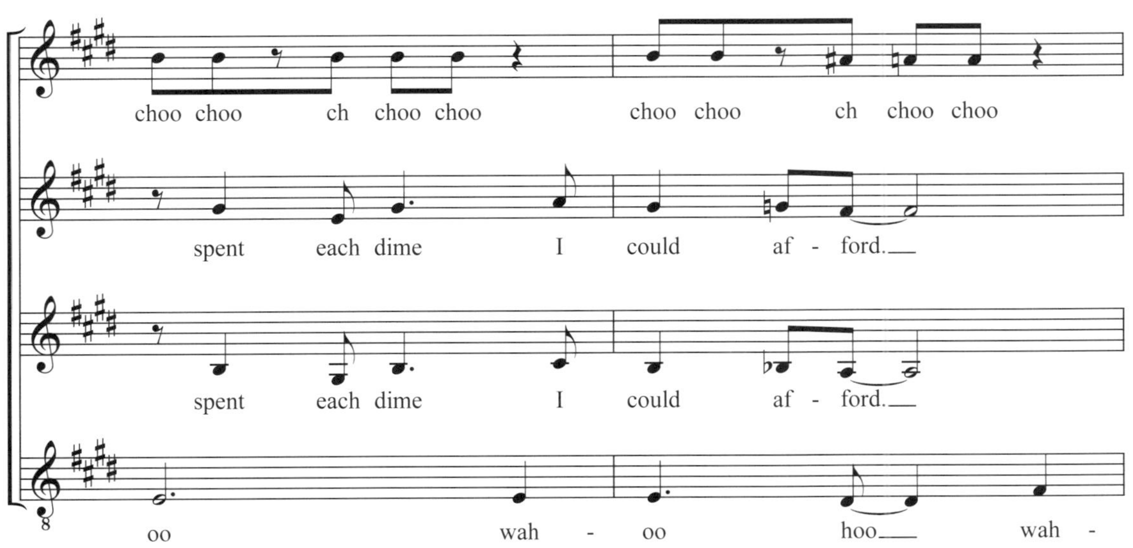
choo choo ch choo choo choo choo ch choo choo
spent each dime I could af - ford.
spent each dime I could af - ford.
oo wah - oo hoo wah -

choo choo ch choo choo   choo choo   ch choo choo   long to hear that
Like   a child   in   wild an-ti-ci-pa-tion,   long to hear that
Like   a child   in   wild an-ti-ci-pa-tion,   long to hear that
oo   an - ti - ci-pa - tion,   hoo________ that
poco a poco cresc.
"All_   a - board."_   Sev - en,___   that's the time we leave, at
"All_   a - board."_   Sev - en,___   that's the time we leave, at
"All_   a - board."_   Sev - en,________
"All   a - board."_   A - board,   Sev - en,________
sev - en.___   I'll be wait-in' up for   Heav - en,___
sev - en.___   I'll be wait-in' up for   Heav - en,___
Sev - en,________   Heav - en,___
Sev - en,________   Heav - en,___

count-in' ev-'ry mile of rail-road track that takes me back.
count-in' ev-'ry mile of rail-road track that takes me back.
count-in' ev-'ry mile of rail-road track that takes me back, oh,
coun-tin' ev-'ry mile, rail-road track that takes me back, oh,
25
woo - woo
Nev-er thought my heart could be so "yearn-y." Why did I de-
Nev-er thought my heart could be so "yearn-y." Why did I de-
Nev-er thought my heart could be so "yearn-y." Why did I de-
29
To Coda
woo - woo
woo - woo
cide to roam? Got-ta take this sen-ti-men-tal jour-ney,
cide to roam? Got-ta take this sen-ti-men-tal jour-ney,
cide to roam? I, Got-ta take this sen-ti-men-tal jour-ney,

D.S. al Coda
At
Sen - ti - men - tal jour - ney home.
Sen - ti - men - tal jour - ney home.
Sen - ti - men - tal jour - ney home. All a
33
lightly
(oo)
Sen - ti - men - tal
Sen - ti - men - tal jour - ney home, Sen - ti - men - tal
Sen - ti - men - tal jour - ney home, Sen - ti - men - tal
Sen - ti - men - tal jour - ney home, Sen - ti - men - tal
jour - ney home, Sen - ti - men - tal jour - ney home.
jour - ney home, Sen - ti - men - tal jour - ney home.
jour - ney home, Sen - ti - men - tal jour - ney home.
jour - ney home, Sen - ti - men - tal jour - ney home.

Dancing in the Streets

Arrangement by
Deke Sharon

Words and Music by
Marvin Gaye, Ivy Hunter and William Stevenson

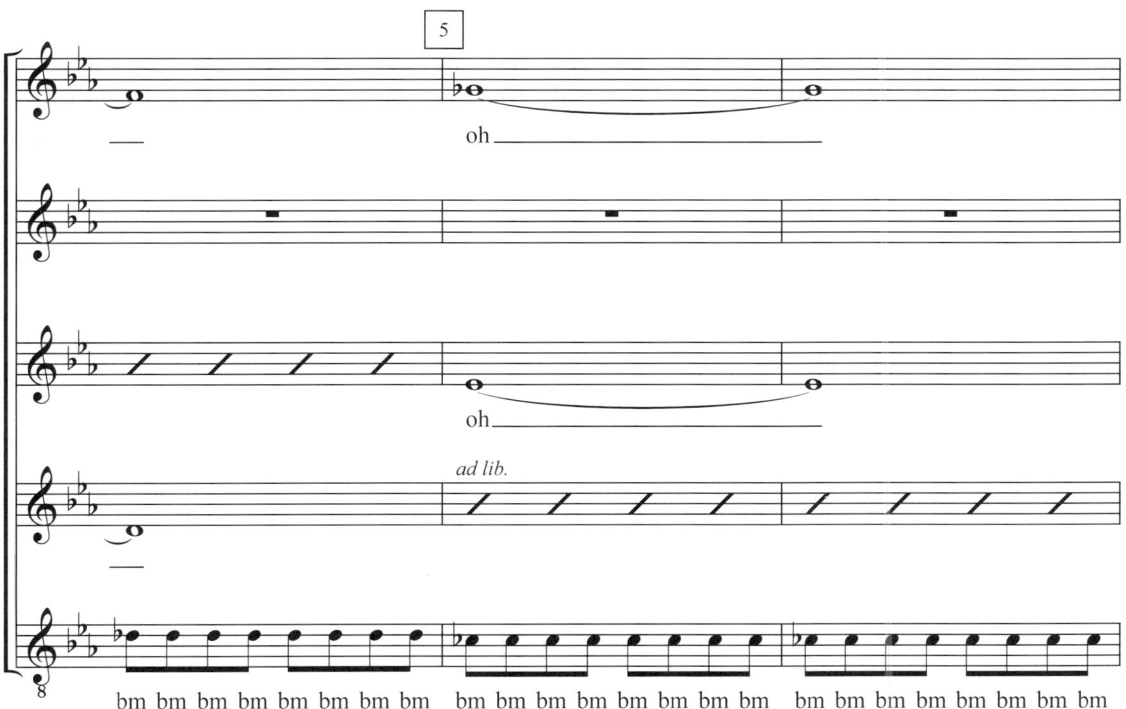

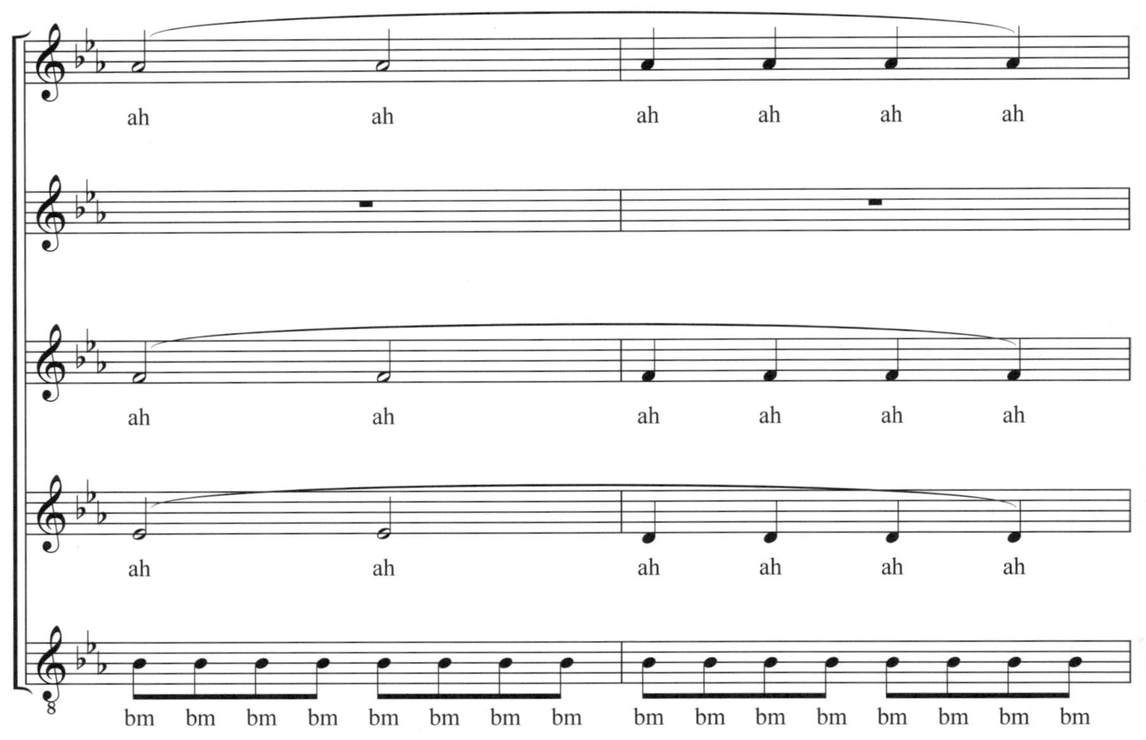
ah ah ah ah ah ah
ah ah ah ah ah ah
ah ah ah ah ah ah
bm bm bm bm bm bm bm bm bm bm bm bm bm bm bm bm

9
mf
oo oo oo hoo a - round the world
oo oo oo hoo a - round the world
mf melody
Call - in' out a - round the world Are you
in - vi - ta - tion a - cross the na - tion, A
mf
oo oo oo hoo a - round the world
oo oo oo hoo a - round the world
mf
oo oo oo hoo a - round the world
oo oo oo hoo a - round the world
mf
doo doo doo doo doo doo doo doo doo doo doo doo

oh ho a brand new beat, There'll be
oh ho the folks to meet,
read-y for a brand new beat? oh hoo
chance for the folks to meet. oh hoo
oh ho a brand new beat, hoo
oh ho the folks to meet, hoo
oh ho a brand new beat, hoo hoo
oh ho the folks to meet, hoo hoo
doo doo doo doo doo doo doo doo doo doo doo doo

13 melody
Sum-mer's here and the time is right for
laugh-in', sing-in', and mu-sic swing-in', And
hoo oh oh oh
hoo oh oh oh
hoo oh oh oh
hoo oh oh oh
hoo oh oh oh for
hoo oh oh oh And
doo doo doo doo doo doo doo doo doo doo doo doo

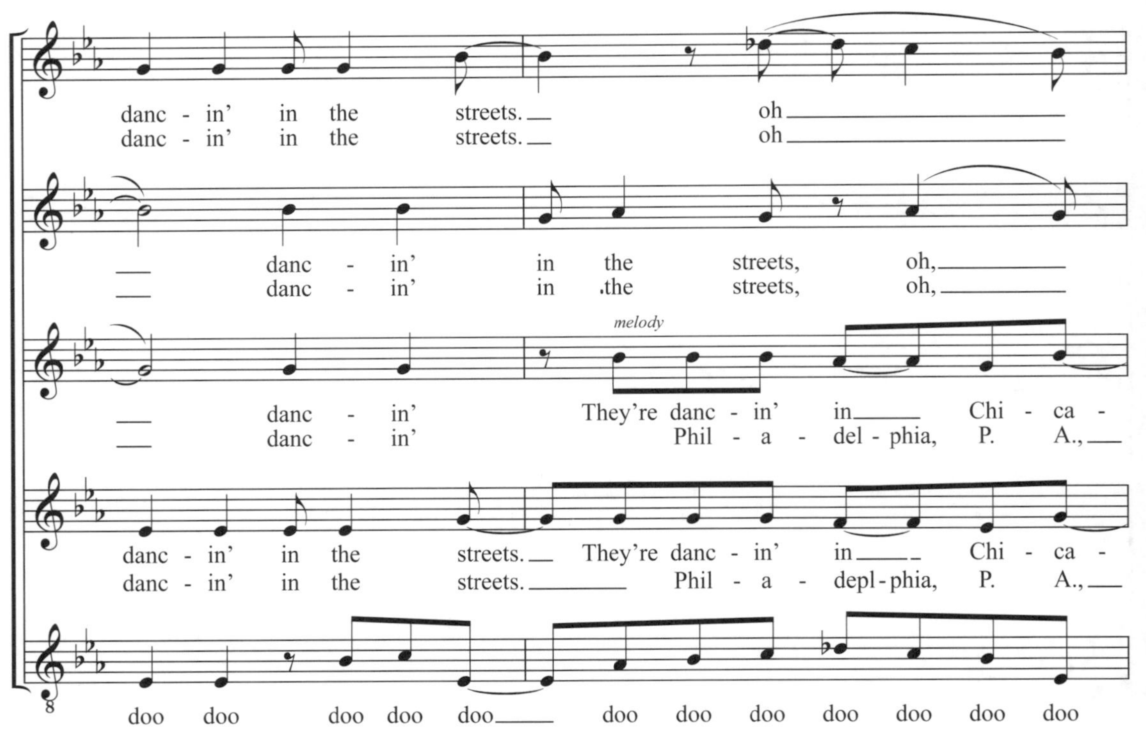
danc - in' in the streets. ___ oh ___
danc - in' in the streets. ___ oh ___
___ danc - in' in the streets, oh, ___
___ danc - in' in .the streets, oh, ___
melody
___ danc - in' They're danc - in' in ___ Chi - ca -
___ danc - in' Phil - a - del - phia, P. A., ___
danc - in' in the streets. ___ They're danc - in' in ___ Chi - ca -
danc - in' in the streets. ___ Phil - a - depl - phia, P. A., ___
doo doo doo doo doo ___ doo doo doo doo doo doo doo

danc - in' in the streets, ___ d dan d dan d dan d
danc - in' in the streets, ___ d dan d dan d dan d
danc - in' in the streets, ___ Down in
danc - in' in the streets, ___ Bal - ti - more and D. C., ___
go, ___ oh oo whoa ___ oo oh oo oh oo, Down in
oh oo whoa, ___ Bal - ti - more and D. C., ___
go, danc - in' in the streets, dan dan
danc - in' in the streets, dan dan
doo doo doo doo doo ___ doo doo doo doo doo doo doo

melody
dan danc - in' in the streets.___ In New York___ Cit -
dan danc - in' in the streets.___ Don't for - get the Mo - tor
New Or - leans,___ oh,_______ In New York___ Cit -
___ now, oh,___ Don't for - get the Mo - tor
New Or - leans,___ danc - in' in the streets, danc - in',
___ now, danc - in' in the streets, danc - in',
d danc - in' in the streets.___ no no no no
d danc - in' in the streets.___ no no no no
doo doo doo doo doo_______ doo doo doo doo doo doo doo

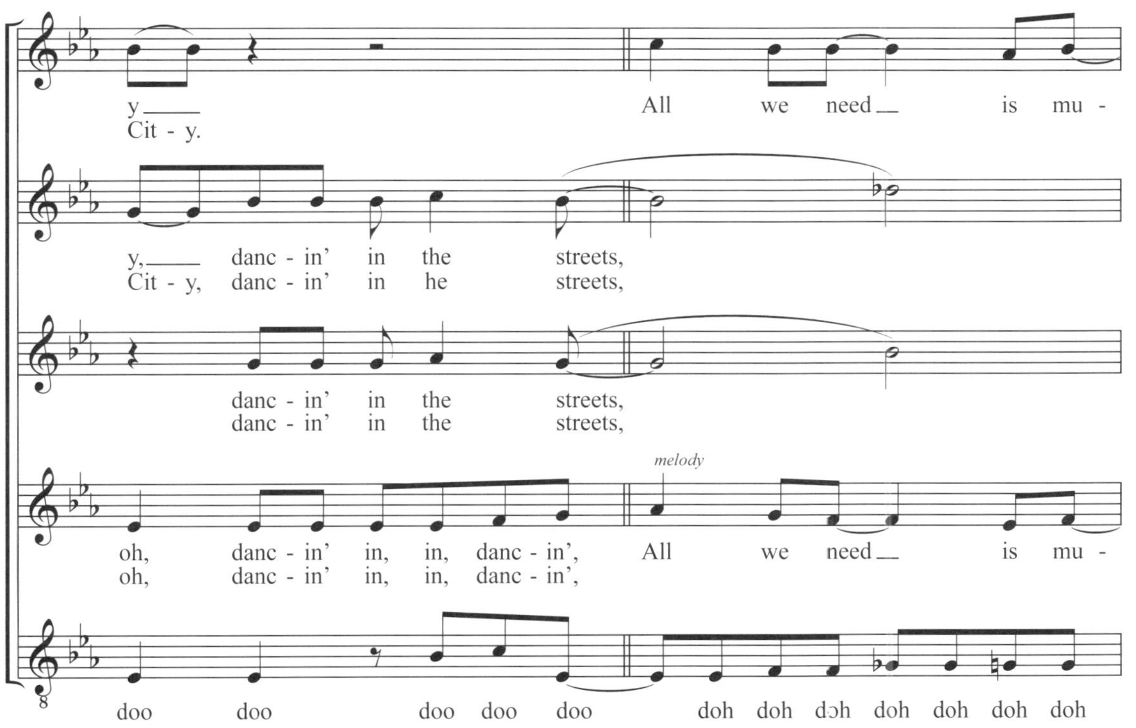
y ____ All we need ___ is mu -
Cit - y.
y,____ danc - in' in the streets,
Cit - y, danc - in' in the streets,
danc - in' in the streets,
danc - in' in the streets,
melody
oh, danc - in' in, in, danc - in', All we need ___ is mu -
oh, danc - in' in, in, danc - in',
doo doo doo doo doo doh doh doh doh doh doh doh

23
sic, sweet mu - sic, There'll be
sweet, sweet, sweet, sweet, mu - sic,
sweet, sweet, sweet, sweet, sweet, mu - sic,
sic, sweet mu - sic, There'll be
doh doh doh doh doh doh doh doh doh doh doh doh doh

mu - sic ev - - - 'ry - where,___ ev - 'ry -
melody
swee - - - - - - ee - ee - ee - eet, There'll be
sweet, sweet, sweet, sweet, sweet, sweet, oo___
mu - sic ev - - - 'ry - where,___ oo___
doh doh doh doh doh doh doh doh doh doh doh

27
where swing-in', sway-in' and rec-ords play-in', And
swing-in', sway - in' and rec-ords play - in', And
doh doh doh doh doh____ doh doh doh doh doh doh doh
danc - in' in the streets, ___ Oh, ___
danc - in' in the streets____ Oh, ___
___ oh oh oo oh oo
danc - in' in the streets, ___ Oh, ___
doh doh doh doh doh____ doh doh doh doh doh doh doh

31
It does - n't mat - ter what you wear, Just as long
oh no no no no no
melody
It does - n't mat - ter what you wear, Just as long
It does - n't mat - ter what you wear, Just as long
dah dah dah dah dah dah dah dah dah dah dah dah dah

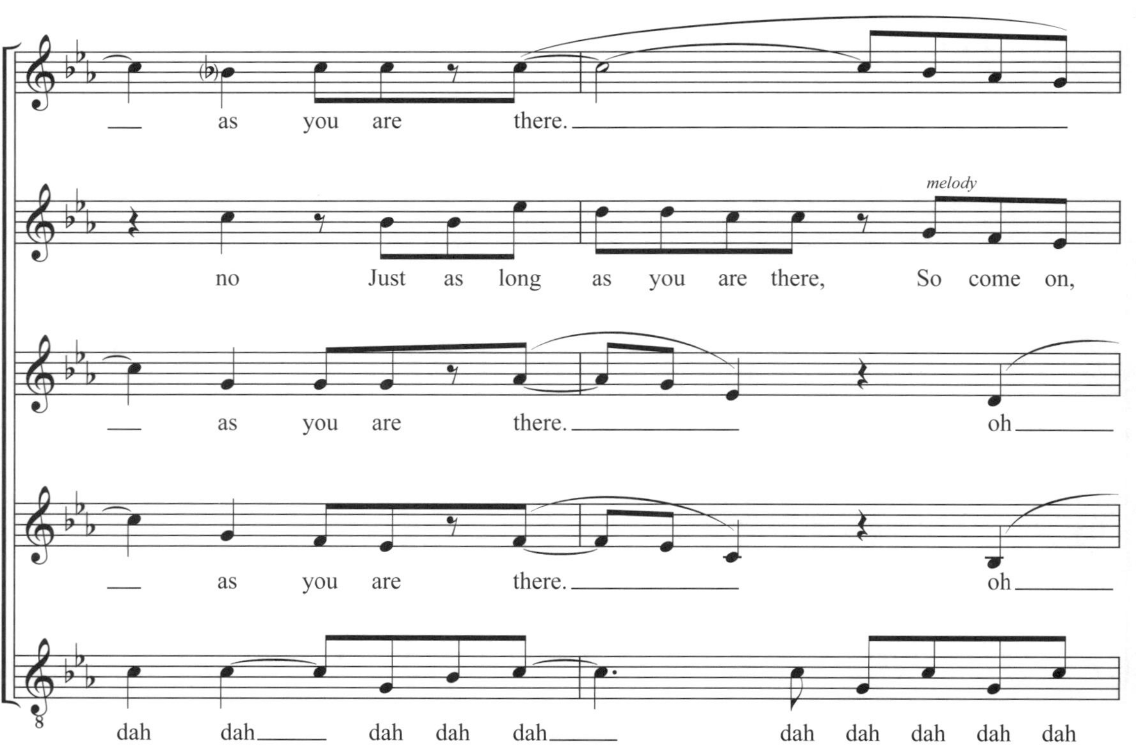
__ as you are there. __
no Just as long as you are there, So come on,
melody
__ as you are there. __ oh __
__ as you are there. __ oh __
dah dah __ dah dah dah __ dah dah dah dah dah

35
f
oh
Ev - 'ry - where a - round
f
ev - 'ry guy grab a girl,
Ev - 'ry - where a - round
f
Ev - 'ry - where,
f
Ev - 'ry - where a - round
f
dah dah dah dah dah dah dah dah dah dah dah dah dah dah dah dah dah dah dah

the world
ah
39
the world, There'll be danc - in',
ah
ev - 'ry - where a - round the world, ah
the world ah
dah dah dah dah dah dah dah dah dah dah dah dah dah

They're danc - in' in the streets, danc - in' in the streets.
ah danc - in' in the streets.
danc - in' in the streets.
danc - in' in the streets.
dah dah dah dah dah dah dah dah dah dah dah dah

danc - in' in the streets.
This is an danc - in' in the streets.
danc - in' in the streets.
danc - in' in the streets.
dah dah dah dah dah dah dah dah dah dah dah dah

Son-Of-A-Preacher Man

Arrangement by
Anne Raugh

Words and Music by
John Hurley and Ronnie Wilkins

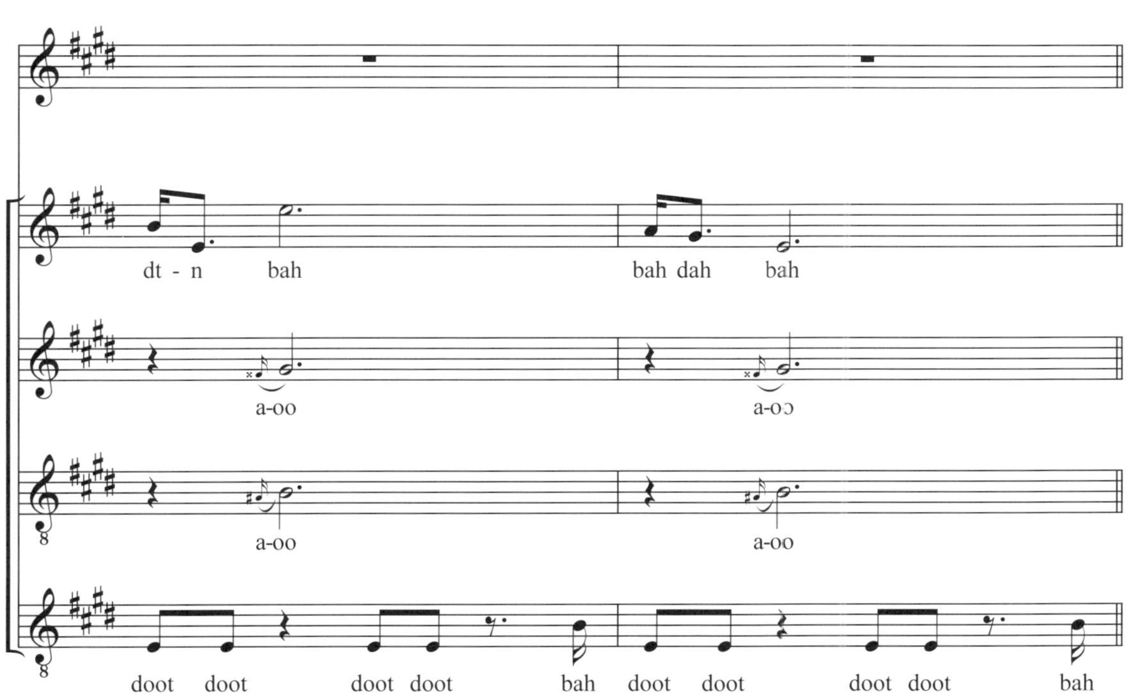

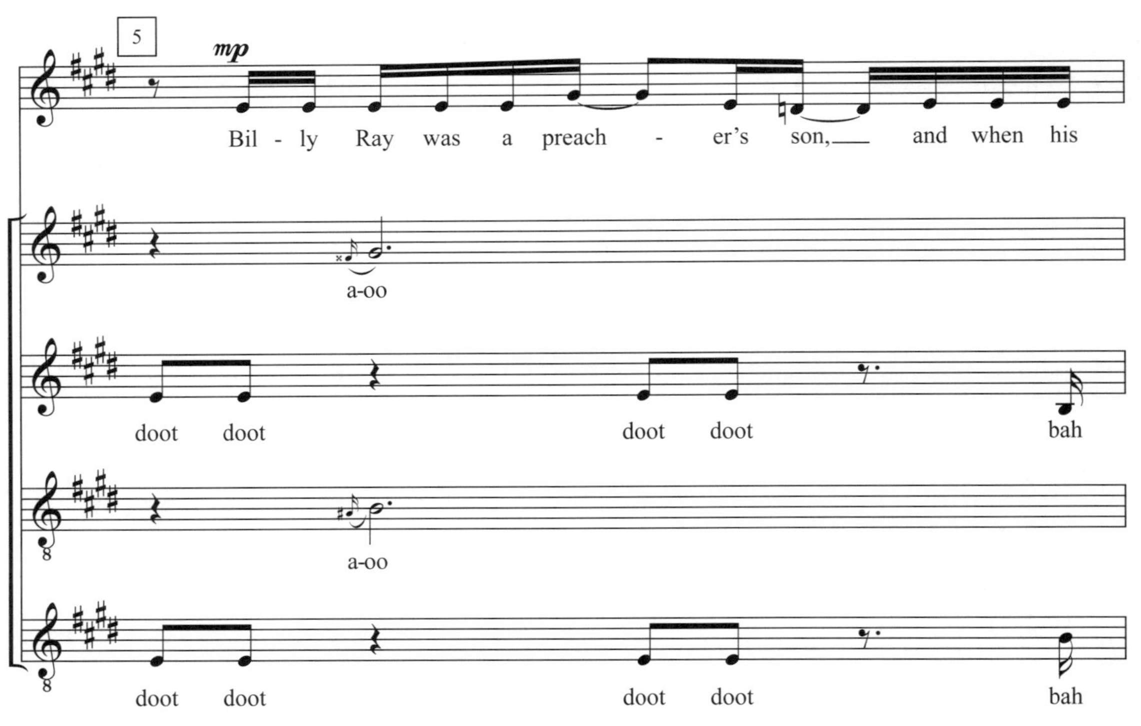
5
mp
Bil - ly Ray was a preach - er's son,___ and when his
a-oo
doot doot doot doot bah
a-oo
doot doot doot doot bah

dad - dy would vis - it he'd come___ a - long.
a-oo hoo___
doot doot doot doot bah
a-oo hoo___
doot doot doot doot bah

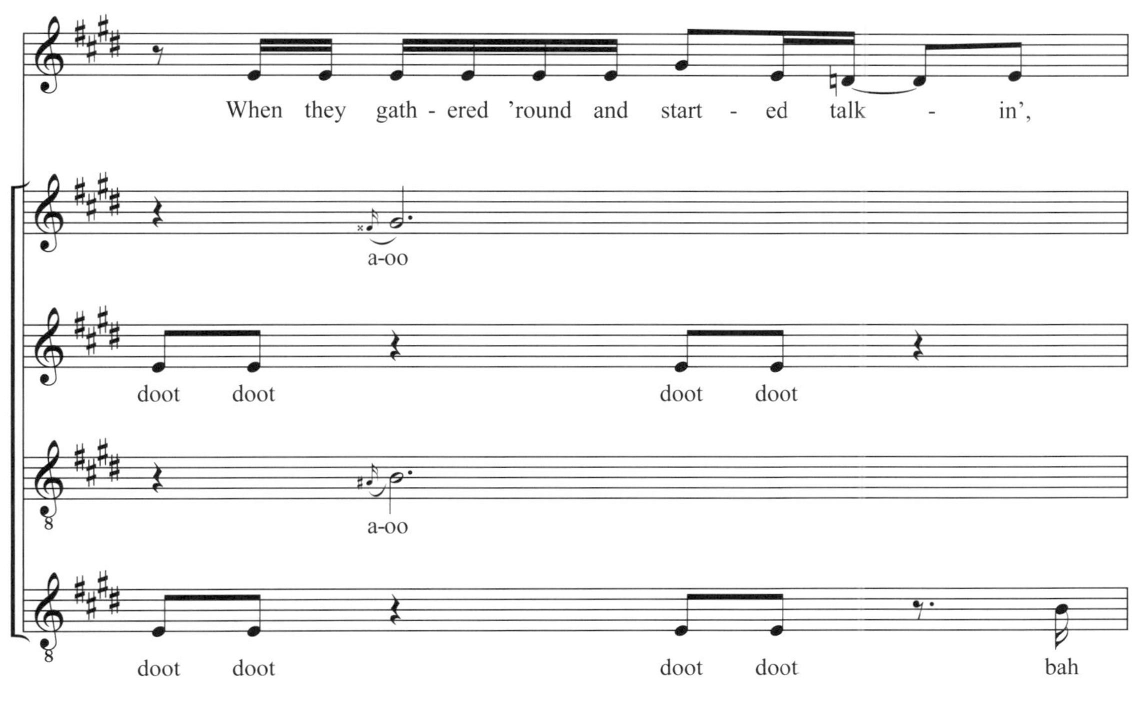
When they gath - ered 'round and start - ed talk - in',
a-oo
doot doot doot doot
a-oo
doot doot bah

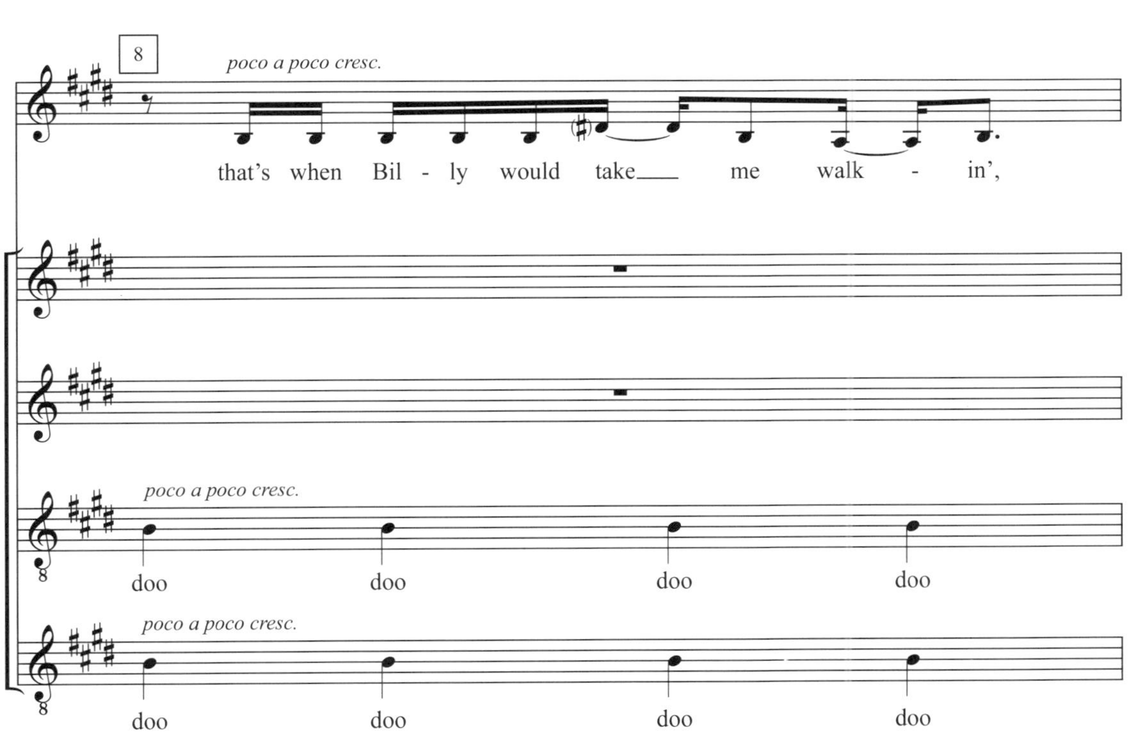
8
poco a poco cresc.
that's when Bil - ly would take___ me walk - in',
poco a poco cresc.
doo doo doo doo
poco a poco cresc.
doo doo doo doo

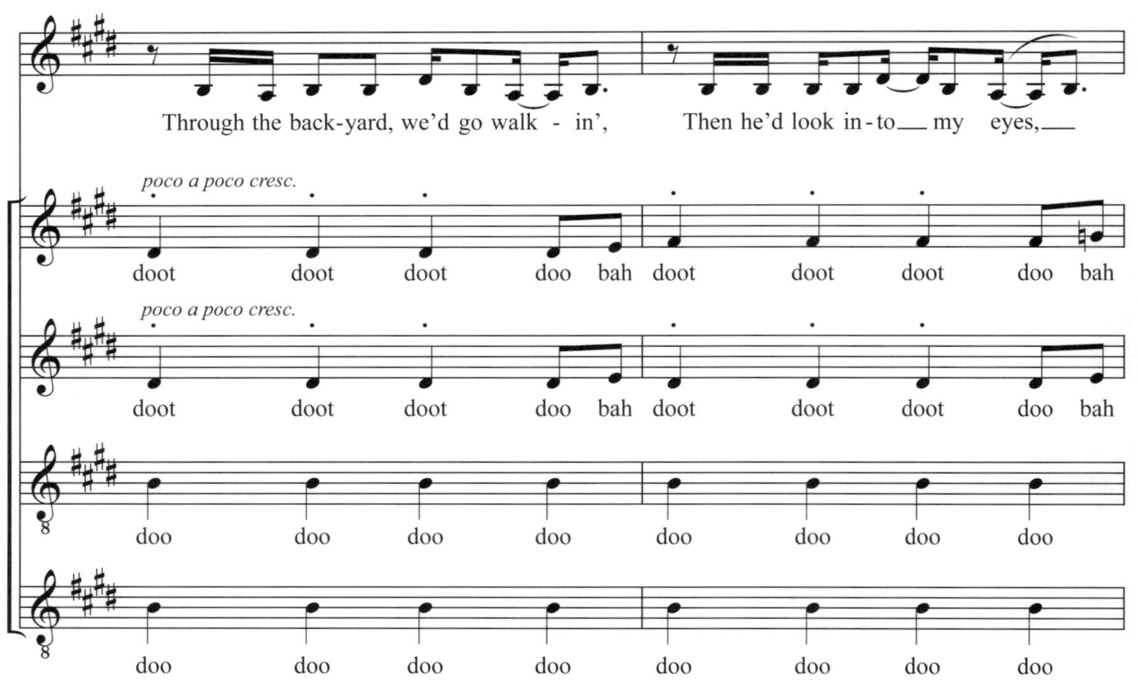
Through the back-yard, we'd go walk - in',
Then he'd look in-to__ my eyes,__
doot doot doot doo bah doot doot doot doo bah
doot doot doot doo bah doot doot doot doo bah
doo doo doo doo doo doo doo doo
doo doo doo doo doo doo doo doo
poco a poco cresc.
poco a poco cresc.

Lord knows, to my_ sur - prise, The on - ly one_ who could ev - er reach_ me
doot doot doot doo on - ly one,_ hoo
doot doot doot doo on - ly one,_ hoo
doo doo doo doo on - ly one,_ hoo
doo doo doo doo, The on - ly one,_ on - ly one,_
mf
mf
mf
mf
mf
12

Was a son of a preach - er man. The on-ly boy_ who could ev -er teach me,
Was a son of a preach - er man._ on-ly boy,_ hoo
Was a son of a preach - er man._ on-ly boy,_ hoo
Was a son of a preach - er man._ on-ly boy,_ hoo
oo, Was a son of a preach - er. Yes the on-ly boy,_ on-ly boy,_

16
Was a son of a preach - er man. Yes he was, he was,_
Was a son of a preach - er man._ oo, he was, yes he
Was a son of a preach - er man._ oo, he was, yes he
Was a son of a preach - er man._ oo, he was, yes he
oo, Was a son of a preach - er, Yes he was, yes he was, yes he

ooo, yes he
was.
was.
was.
was, doo doo doo bah doot doot doot doot bah
bah dahp bah
doo dt doo
doo dt doo

Be-in' good is-n't al - ways eas - y,
bah dahp bah doot doot doo
doo dt doo doot doot bah
doo dt doo doot doot doo
doot doot doot doot bah doot doot doot doot bah

No mat-ter how hard I'd try. When he start-ed sweet talk - in' to me,
doot doot doo wah - oo doot doot doo
doot doot doot doot bah doot doot doot doot
doot doot doo wah - oo doot doot doo
doot doot doot doot bah doot doot doot doot bah

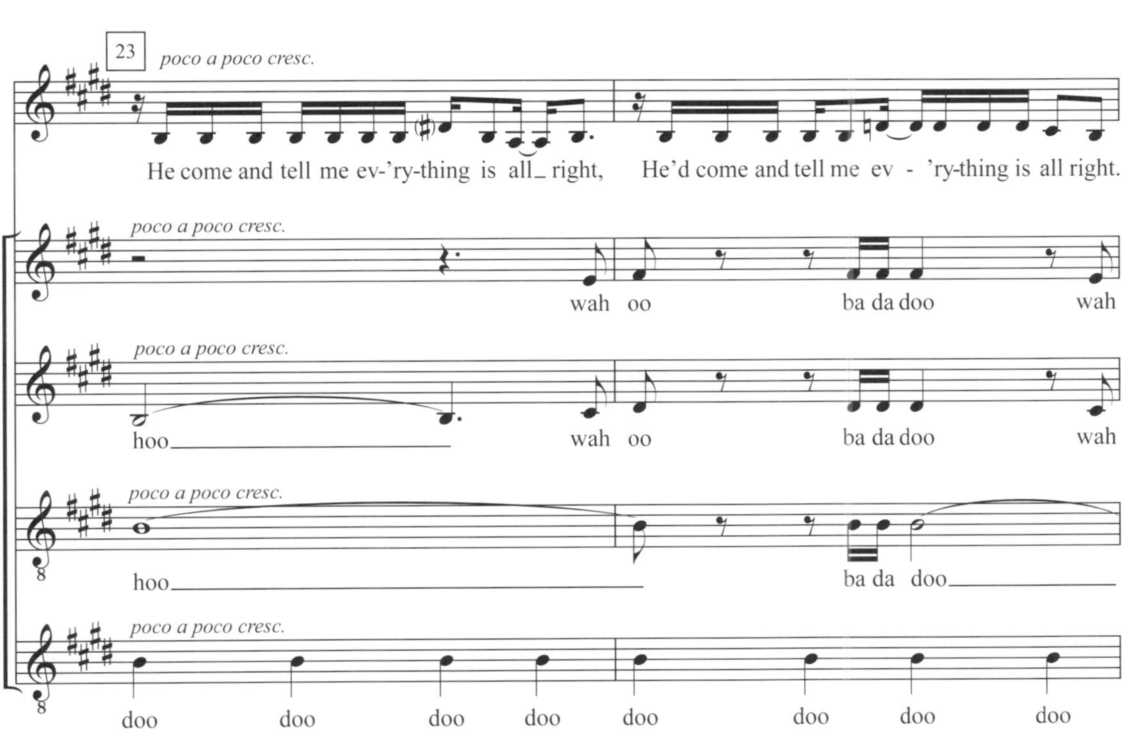

23
poco a poco cresc.
He come and tell me ev-'ry-thing is all right, He'd come and tell me ev - 'ry-thing is all right.
poco a poco cresc.
wah oo ba da doo wah
poco a poco cresc.
hoo wah oo ba da doo wah
poco a poco cresc.
hoo ba da doo
poco a poco cresc.
doo doo doo doo doo doo doo doo

mf
26
Can I get a-way a-gain to - night? The on-ly one_ who could ev-er reach me
oo bah dah doo Yes the on-ly one,_ oo wah
oo bah dah doo Yes the on-ly one,_ oo wah
_ bah dah doo Yes the on-ly one,_ oo wah
doo doo doo Yes the on-ly one,_ on-ly one,_

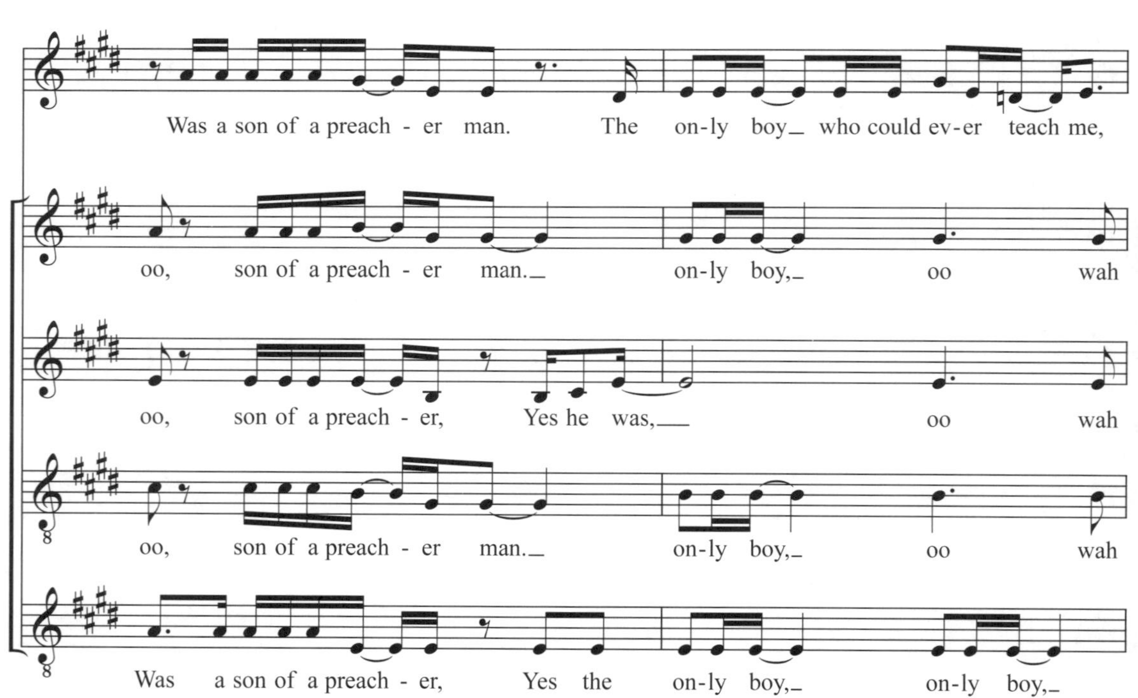
Was a son of a preach - er man. The on-ly boy_ who could ev-er teach me,
oo, son of a preach - er man._ on-ly boy,_ oo wah
oo, son of a preach - er, Yes he was,__ oo wah
oo, son of a preach - er man._ on-ly boy,_ oo wah
Was a son of a preach - er, Yes the on-ly boy,_ on-ly boy,_

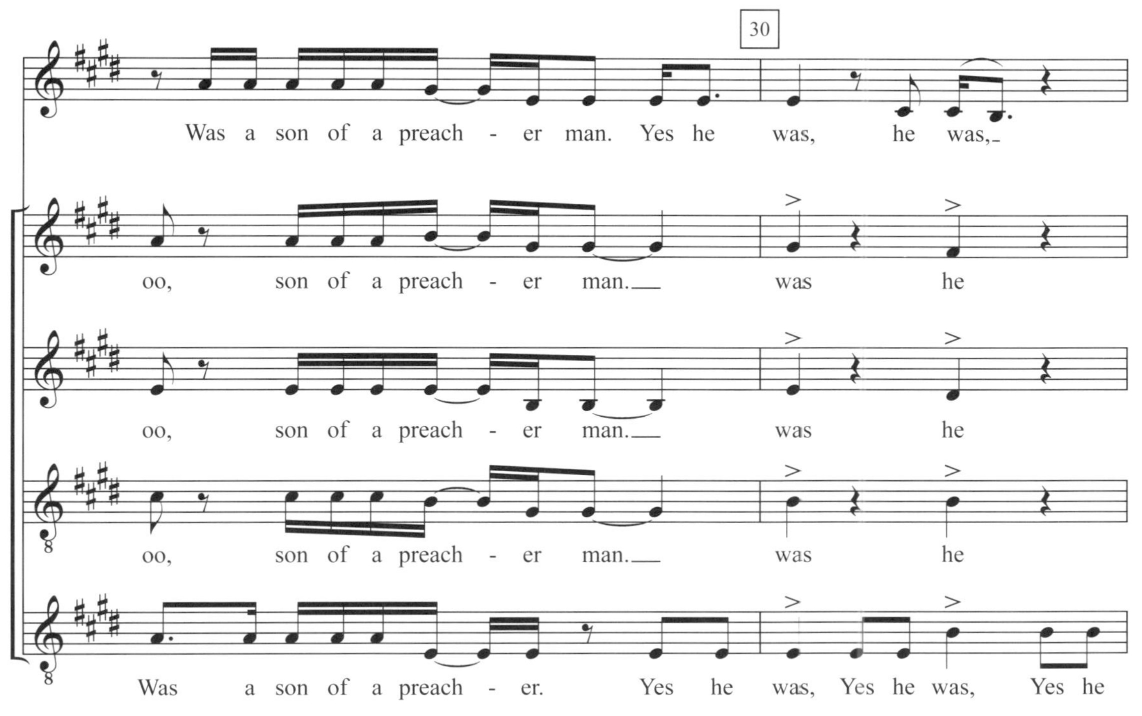
30
Was a son of a preach - er man. Yes he was, he was,
oo, son of a preach - er man. was he
oo, son of a preach - er man. was he
oo, son of a preach - er man. was he
Was a son of a preach - er. Yes he was, Yes he was, Yes he

32
ooo, yes he was.
was, Yes he was, doo doo doot doot doot bah
was, Yes he was, doo doo doot doot doot bah
was, Yes he was, doo doo doot doot doot bah
was, doo doo, doot doo doot doo bah dt - n doo bah

How well I re-mem - ber, The look_ was in his eyes._
doo doot doo doot doot_ doot doo wah bah doot doo doot doot
doo doot doo doot doot_ doot doo wah bah doot doo doot doot
doo doot doo doot doot_ doot doo wah bah doot doo doot doot
doot doo_ bah doo doo doot doo_____ bah dt - n doo_____ bah

Steal-in' kiss-es from me_ on the sly._ Tak-in' time to make_ time,
wah doo_ doo doo wah_______ make_ time,_
wah doo_ doo doo wah_______ make_ time,_
wah doo_ doo doo wah_______ make_ time,_
doot doo_____ bah doo doo doo doo doot doo_____ bah doot doo_ bah dt-n

Tell-in' me that he's all___ mine,
Learn-in' from each oth - er's know - in',
oo___________ all___ mine,___
Learn-in' from each oth - er's know - in',
oo___________ all___ mine,___ oh,
oo___________ all___ mine,___ oh,
doot doo___ bah doot doo_ bah dt-n doot doo_______ bah doot doo___

cresc.
Look - in' to see___ how much___ we've grown,_ And the
cresc.
Look - in' to see___ how much___ we've grown,_
cresc.
Look - in' to see___ how much,___ The
cresc.
Look - in' to see___ how much,___ The
cresc.
doo bah doo bah doot doot doo bah doo

on-ly one_ who could ev-er reach me Was a son of a preach - er man. The
on-ly one,_ hoo wah oo, son of a preach - er man,_
on-ly one,_ hoo wah oo, son of a preach - er, Yes he was,.
on-ly one,_ hoo wah oo, son of a preach - er man,_
on-ly one,_ on-ly one,_ oo, Was a son of a preach - er. Yes the

on-ly boy_ who could ev-er teach me Was the son of a preach - er man, yes he was,
on-ly boy,_ hoo wah oo son of a preach - er man,_
_ hoo wah oo son of a preach - er, Yes he was_
on-ly boy,_ hoo wah oo son of a preach - er man,_
on-ly boy,_ on-ly boy,_ oo, Was a son of a preach - er. Yes he

Vamp for solo
Solo ad lib.

Repeat
Repeat
on-ly boy__ who could ev-er reach__ me, Was a son of a preach - er man.__ The
on-ly boy__ who could ev-er reach__ me, Was a son of a preach - er man.__ The
on-ly boy,__ yes he was,______ preach - er man,__ The
on-ly boy,__ and the on-ly boy,__ he was a son of a preach - er. Lord, and the

Last Time
Last Time
Was a son of a preach - er man, Yes he was,__ yes he was, Lord, he was.__ Yes he was.
Was a son of a preach - er man, Yes he was,__ yes he was, Lord, he was. Yes he was.
was,______ preach - er man, Yes he was,__ yes he was, Lord, he was. Yes he was.
was a son of a preach - er, Yes he was,__ yes he was, Lord, he was. Yes he was.

Ain't No Mountain High Enough

Arrangement by
Anne Raugh and Deke Sharon

Words and Music by
Nickolas Ashford and Valerie Simpson

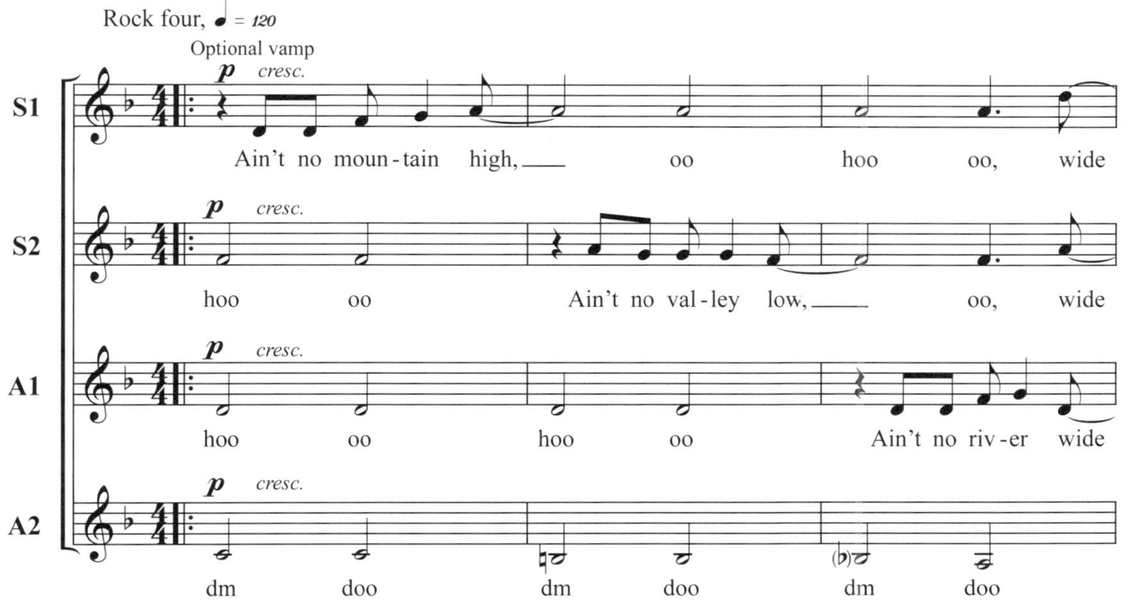

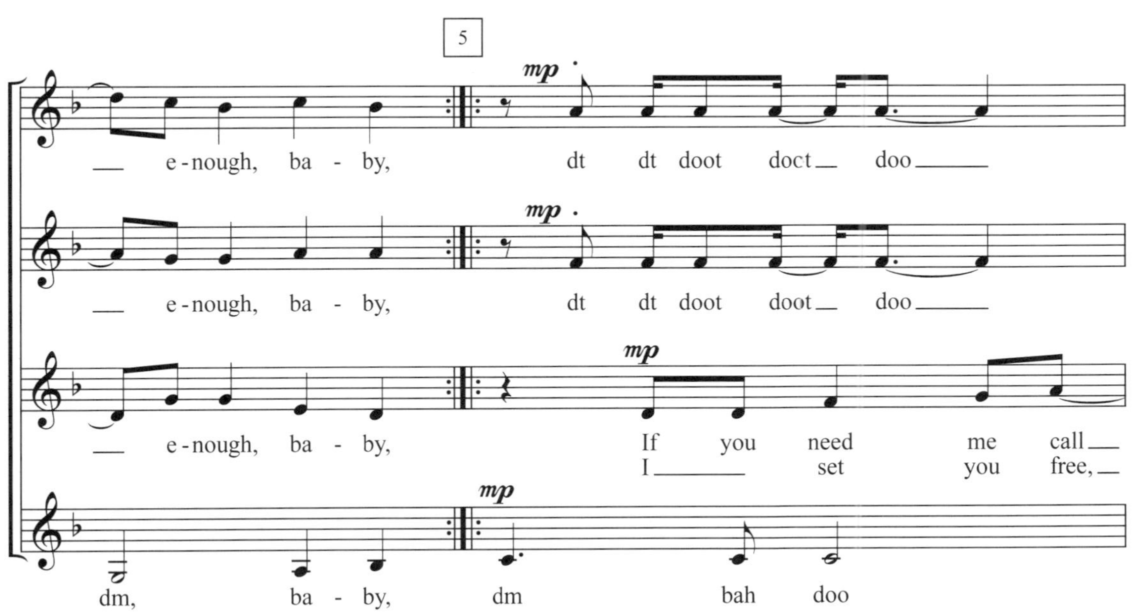

dt dt doot doot doo dt dt doot doot doo
dt dt doot doot doo dt dt doot doot doo
me, no mat - ter where you are, no mat - ter how
I told you you could al - ways count on me.
dm bah doo dm bah doo
9 cresc.
dt doo doot doo doo dt dt doot doot doo
cresc.
dt doo doot doo doo dt dt doot doot doo
cresc.
far; From that day on, I made a vow,
Just call my name,
cresc.
dm bah doo doo dm bah doo
dt dt doot doot doo dt dt doot doot doo
dt dt doot doot doo dt dt doot doot doo
I'll be there in a hur - ry, You don't have to wor -
I'll be there when you want me, Some way, some how,
dm bah doo dm bah doo

'Cause ba - by there ain't no moun - tain high
'Cause ba - by there ain't no moun - tain high
- ry, 'Cause ba - by there ain't no moun - tain,
'Cause ba - by there
dm, 'Cause ba - by there ain't no moun - tain,
e - nough, Ain't no val - ley low
e - nough, Ain't no val - ley low
ain't no moun - tain high e - nough, no there ain't no val - ley,
ain't no moun - tain high e - nough, no there ain't no val - ley,
e - nough, Ain't no riv - er wide
e - nough, Ain't no riv - er wide
ain't no val - ley low e - nough, and there ain't no riv - er,
ain't no val - ley low e - nough, and there ain't no riv - er,

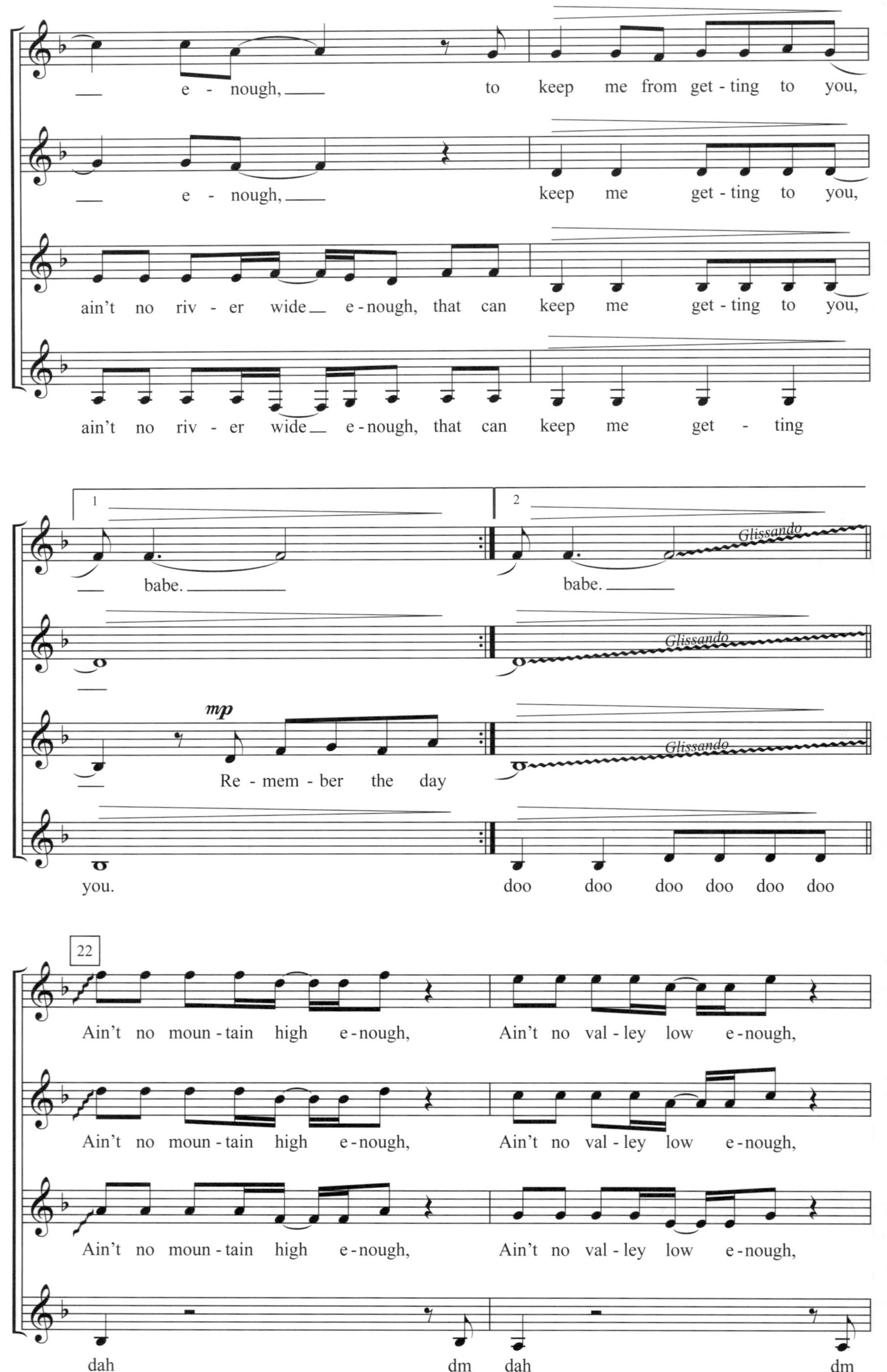
e - nough, to keep me from get - ting to you,
e - nough, keep me get - ting to you,
ain't no riv - er wide e - nough, that can keep me get - ting to you,
ain't no riv - er wide e - nough, that can keep me get - ting
babe.
babe.
Glissando
Glissando
Glissando
mp
Re - mem - ber the day
you.
doo doo doo doo doo doo
Ain't no moun - tain high e - nough, Ain't no val - ley low e - nough,
Ain't no moun - tain high e - nough, Ain't no val - ley low e - nough,
Ain't no moun - tain high e - nough, Ain't no val - ley low e - nough,
dah dm dah dm

Ain't no riv-er wide e-nough to keep me from you.
Ain't no riv-er wide e-nough to keep me from you.
Ain't no riv-er wide e-nough to keep me from you.
dah dm dah dah dm ba da
Ain't no moun-tain high e-nough, Ain't no val-ley low e-nough,
Ain't no moun-tain high e-nough, Ain't no val-ley low e-nough,
Ain't no moun-tain high e-nough, Ain't no val-ley low e-nough,
dah dm d dah dah dm d dah
Ain't no riv-er wide e-nough to keep me from you.
Ain't no riv-er wide e-nough to keep me from you.
Ain't no riv-er wide e-nough to keep me from you.
dah dm d dah dah dah dm ba da

40
30
Ain't no moun - tain high e - nough, Ain't no val - ley low e - nough,
Ain't no moun - tain high e - nough,
Ain't no moun - tain high e - nough, Ain't no val - ley low e - nough,
ain't no moun - tain high e - nough, no there
34
Ain't no riv - er wide e - nough to keep me from you. Ain't no riv - er
Ain't no val - ley low e - nough, Ain't no riv - er
Ain't no riv - er wide e - nough to keep me from you. Ain't no riv - er
Ain't no val - ley low e - nough, and there Ain't no riv - er
molto rit. Slowly
wide e - nough... To keep me from get - ting you.
wide e - nough... hoo hoo Ain't no moun - tain high e - nough.
wide e - nough... hoo hoo Ain't no moun - tain high e - nough.
wide e - nough... hoo hoo Ain't no moun - tain high e - nough.

PERFORMANCE NOTES

As with all our songbooks, we believe that an arrangement isn't finished until a group makes it their own. Don't hesitate to change notes, add an additional part or some vocal percussion, or alter it in any other way to fit your group perfectly. We did our best to distill each melody line down to an easily readable voice part, but the result is only an approximation of the original. In each case, refer to the original song, if available, or at least feel free to push and pull the rhythms and pitches to make it your own.

These arrangements are written in four or five parts, but there is a tacit assumption that those voices are of equal strength. As you work on each arrangement, listen carefully to the balance – especially in the lower voices. Female voices tend to lose resonance drastically as they approach the bottom of their range. So as a general rule, if more than four voices are available they should be added from the bottom up. For the same reason, transposing an arrangement up one or two steps can also have a dramatic impact on balance.

Respect: The key to tuning the chords in this song is to get the tritone intervals (E to B-flat and E-flat to A in the soprano accompaniment voices) consistently and solidly in tune. Fortunately, this harsh-sounding interval is relatively easy to tune once you've gotten used to what it's supposed to sound like. This is a place where practicing this specific interval by singing with a piano or guitar can help you rapidly develop an ear for the sound. When you're comfortable with the harmony, you can really dig into the background figures and strike them quickly and confidently, which is just what this arrangement needs to produce a funky, bluesy groove.

Sentimental Journey: Be wary of rushing this song – it's a sweet, nostalgic ballad. But at the same time, avoid letting the tempo drag down into lullabye range. A happy, upbeat energy in the accompaniment with lots of emphasis on the diction will help balance things out nicely. Yes, those *choo-choos* and *woo-woos* are supposed to sound kind of like train sounds; play with them until you get the sound and feel that works for you.

Dancing in the Streets: The key to this song is to continually pull the melody to the forefront by making sure every singer knows when she's singing lead, when she's singing a duet with the lead, and when she's singing a background part. In addition, don't let the syncopation (especially anticipations) throw off the groove or cause the whole group to accelerate.

Son-Of-A-Preacher Man: This arrangement starts simply and builds all the way through to the end, so take care to avoid the temptation to throw everything you've got into the first or second chorus section. The soprano 1 line in mm. 1-4 and 19-20 can and probably should be bent and twisted to mimic a blues guitar or saxophone line. The more clearly and percussively the background figures are sung, the more intensity they will carry *without* having to increase the volume.

Ain't No Mountain High Enough: This is a fairly simple, straight-up arrangement that starts calmly and builds to a dramatic climax in mm. 22-30. Keep the background figures clean and you can't go wrong – but by all means experiment as the mood takes you. From m. 22 on, for example, you can play with the dynamics to fit your group's style and any choreography you might have. Similarly, the last four measures can be interpreted in a number of different ways, from a full-*forte* with an extended soprano melisma in the last measure, to a sudden, surprise *mezzo-piano* if you want a more soulful bridge into your next tune.

WHAT IS CASA?

The Contemporary A Cappella Society
is a non-profit organization formed in 1990 to foster and promote a cappella music. We serve both the fan and the performer.

Membership Levels

BASIC: For $35 a year ($40 outside the U.S., $25 with student ID), you get a subscription to the Contemporary A Cappella News (CAN), a bi-monthly magazine that includes international news and concert calendars, guest columns by big names in the a cappella industry, interviews with top groups, how-to articles, advertising and album reviews.

PREMIUM: If you're in a group or serious about a cappella, you'll want this level. For $50 a year ($55 outside the U.S., $35 with student ID) you'll get the CAN and one free classified ad in it, plus all of CASA's group services (the group directory, telephone consultation, discounts with a cappella businesses, etc.). Other members of your group can get their own copies of the CAN for an additional $10 per member.

SPONSOR: For $100 ($110 outside the U.S.), in addition to all the Premium level benefits you also get your own copy of A Cappella Radio International (ARI) each month.

BENEFACTOR: For $250 ($260 outside the U.S.), you get all the Sponsor level benefits *and* hot-off-the-presses copies of this year's BOCA and CARA CDs, and one other CASA-published CD.

CASA Productions

- The **Urban Harmony Movement**, a free community enhancing singing programs for teens and adults
- The **A Cappella Summit**, which brings hundreds of fans, performers and enthusiasts together for two days of seminars, concerts and workshops.
- The **Contemporary A Cappella Recording Awards**, a yearly quest for the best recorded a cappella music from around the globe
- **A Cappella Community Awards**, allowing fans to vote for their favorite groups
- The **Northern Harmony** Canadian a cappella festival and competition
- The **International Championship of Collegiate A Cappella**, a competition involving college groups of all styles from across the country
- The **A Cappella Almanac**, the complete a cappella website with links to all CASA programs and everything else you might want to know about a cappella
- The **International A Cappella Recording Archives**, a library of over 3,000 a cappella recordings
- **A Cappella Radio International**, a monthly program of news and interviews, broadcast internationally and on the World Wide Web
- **Contemporary A Cappella Recording Awards CD**, including the best submissions from nominees and winners
- **The Urban Harmony Movement R&B CD**, featuring professional and collegiate groups
- The **Northern Harmony CD**, featuring performances from the inaugural year of that festival
- The **Best of College A Cappella (BOCA) CD** series, produced jointly with Mainely A Cappella
- **Class Notes: The Best of High School A Cappella CD**, a compilation of outstanding high school groups

- The **Definitive A Cappella Press Kit**, a guide for groups putting together their own promotional material
- **Producing the Ultimate A Cappella Show**, a how-to manual covering everything from single-group concerts to festivals
- **Starting an A Cappella Group**, a basic guide to starting up your own group for fun or profit

TO JOIN, send a check to:

CASA
2525 Van Ness Ave, Suite 205
San Francisco, CA 94109
USA

For more information, drop us a line:

Phone: 1.415.563.5224
Fax: 1.415.921.2834
Email: casa@casa.org
World Wide Web: http://www.casa.org/

TOTAL VOCAL
perfect harmony, one note at a time

Total Vocal is a company specializing in a cappella and vocal services, including:

- **Arranging**: We can provide your group with custom arrangements, published sheet music, and arranging advice. We're responsible for over 1,000 vocal arrangements in a wide array of voicings and styles, for high school, collegiate, professional and recreational groups.

> *"A battery of sounds that make mincemeat of the traditional limits of the human voice"*
> – The *Oakland Tribune*

> *"You're going to have a serious impact on the future of choral music."*
> – Kirby Shaw

- **Producing**: We can help you produce a great album, from planning and preproduction to recording, mixing and distribution. Our clients range from classical to doo-wop to pop, from high school to cutting-edge professionals.

> *"The best pure quality a cappella recording I've ever heard."*
> – Elie Landau, *Recorded A Cappella Review Board*

> *"Stellar Production Work"*
> –Mainely A Cappella

- **Directing**: We can help you form an a cappella group or other vocal music project, direct it through the initial start-up phase, and provide music direction on an ongoing basis.

> *"Soulful melodies, crashing drums, driving bass: you won't believe your ears."*
> – The New York Times

> *"Sensational Sounds! You give a whole new meaning to the word 'acappella'."*
> – Ed McMahon

- **Teaching**: We provide a number of educational services for individuals and groups on a one-time or ongoing basis, including workshops, informational booklets, group coaching and private lessons.

> *"Nothing short of wonderful; just the right mix of expertise, experience, communication skills and charisma"*
> – Colorado Vocal Jazz Society

> *"Il maestro di a cappella populare"*
> – Daigo Music School, Italy

For more information, contact:

Deke Sharon, President
Total Vocal
681 10th Avenuet
San Francisco, CA 94118
Phone: 1.415.846.4073
Email: info@totalvocal.com
URL: http://www.totalvocal.com/

Other A Cappella Resources

MAINELY A CAPPELLA (MAC)
MAC is a mail-order catalog published annually with quarterly updates. It features more than 3,000 titles, including rare and international releases. The catalog represents a wide range of styles and genres - from the latest in pop, jazz and world bands to classical ensembles and barbershop harmonies.

MAC Yak
Mainely A CAPPELLA'S electronic newsletter features new releases, pre-releases, and is the only place to find great sale items.

VARSITY VOCALS
Varsity Vocals is a student a cappella outreach organization that sponsors four great programs:

The *Best of College A Cappella (BOCA)* annual compilation CD encourages college groups to compete for a place on this sought-after CD.

The *International Championship of Collegiate A Cappella (ICCA)* brings together hundreds of college a cappella singers who compete in regional concerts across North America for a place in the national finals, held in the Avery Fisher Hall of Lincoln Center, New York City.

The *Best of High School A Cappella (BOHSA)* compilation CD features high school groups from all over the world.

The *Varsity Vocals Scholarship* is a separate non-profit fund that recognizes college students who are advancing the growth of *a cappella*.

For more details see: *www.varsityvocals.com*

ON-LINE COMMUNITY
The Mainely A CAPPELLA catalog has a popular home page on the World Wide Web, at *www.a–cappella.com*. There are more than 10,000 RealAudio® and MP3 sound clips to hear, an extensive and continually updated concert calendar, and secure on-line buying. There is also a very active newsgroup on the Internet designed exclusively for a cappella fans: *rec.music.a–cappella* (on the web at *groups.google.com*).

For more information contact us:

PO Box 159
Southwest Harbor, ME 04679
Phone: 1.800.827.2936
International: 1.207.244.7603
Fax: 1.207.244.7613
Email: catalog@a-cappella.com
World Wide Web: www.a-cappella.com
For a FREE catalog call: 1.800.827.2936

Other Titles Available from
Contemporary A Cappella Publishing

Contemporary A Cappella Publishing (CAP) produces the Contemporary A Cappella Songbook Collection:

SATB Series
Volume 1	HL08741649	*
Volume 2	HL08741650	*
A CASA Christmas	HL08741651	*
Songs for All Occasions	HL08742050	
I Feel Good	HL08742598	*
Shout	HL08743512	
Love Songs A Cappella	HL08743515	

SSAA Series
Natural Woman	HL08742904
Girls Just Want to Have Fun	*coming in 2004*
Respect	*coming in 2004*

TTBB Series
Good Ol' A Cappella	HL08743513
Sh-Boom	HL08743514

SAB Series
Under the Boardwalk	*coming in 2004*
Deck the Hall	*coming in 2004*

Jazz Series
Standards	HL08743235
Classics	*coming in 2004*

Performer Series
Continuum: The First Songbook of Sweet Honey in the Rock	HL08742029
Ticket to Ride: The Swingle Singers	HL08743854

These, in addition to *The Collegiate A Cappella Arranging Manual* (HL0874259), are available wherever songbooks are sold, or online at *www.a-cappella.com* and *www.casa.org*.

Contemporary A Cappella Publishing, Inc.
P.O. Box 159 · Southwest Harbour, ME 04679
www.capublish.com

* Part-predominant learning tapes and CDs are available for the arrangements in these volumes directly from Mainely A CAPPELLA. Call 1.800.827.2936, email *order@a-cappella.com* or order online at *www.a-cappella.com* and specify Soprano, Alto, Tenor, Bass, or a set of all four.